Item #1013735203
click to bid

Item #1000286349
click to bid

Item #1604208730
click to bid

Item #1151635234
click to bid

Item #1470683814
click to bid

Item #1440316227
click to bid

Item #1143331859
click to bid

click to bid

click to bid

Item #1000361119
click to bid

Item #1000268749
click to bid

Item #1169632432
click to bid

Item #1000285154
click to bid

Item #8369220734
click to bid

Item #2322001912
click to bid

Item #1156227138
click to bid

Item #1601038615
click to bid

Item #1606774254
click to bid

Item #1000282679
click to bid

Item #1470683814
click to bid

Item #1000276525
click to bid

Item #1000307692
click to bid

Item #1408821408
click to bid

Item #1000303938
click to bid

Item #1658669743
click to bid

D0360145

DEDICATED TO PAPA.
THANKS.

Thanks to Liz Steger for all her support, patience, and wonderful photography; Chris Steighner for making this happen; Headcase Design for pulling it all together; Johnny Fox for getting me hooked on eBay; Bobby at the Hoboken post office for making sure I got all my packages; the many eBayers who were great sports and very helpful— particularly those who donated or loaned me merchandise; Dad for going to a complete stranger's house and taking a picture of firewood and Mom for making me the collector I am today.

First published in the United States of America in 2002 by UNIVERSE PUBLISHING
A Division of Rizzoli International Publications, Inc.
300 Park Avenue South, New York, NY 10010

2002 2003 2004 2005 2006 2007/
10 9 8 7 6 5 4 3 2 1

Printed in Hong Kong

Library of Congress Catalog Card Number:
2001099804

DESIGN:
Paul Kepple and Timothy Crawford
@ Headcase Design

PHOTO CREDITS:
Thomas Aloisio, p. 95 bottom left; Vincent P. Benabese, p. 39 bottom; Bette Blackwell, p. 81; Dan Bravender, p. 55 top left; Josh Capps, p.78 right; Mark Frierson, p. 72 left; Helen Hall, p. 95 top; Paul Hartzman, p. 106 left; Erica Horak, p. 100; Kurt Hueneke, p. 102; Greg Kasen, p. 73 bottom left; James Larson, p. 55 top right; Jeff Lesssard, p. 49 bottom left; Char Leverette, p. 78 left; Susie Littrell, p. 104; Jeff Misavice, p. 62 right; Steve Molla, p. 80 bottom; Michael R. Myers, p. 80 top; Allan Nobles, p. 95 bottom right; R. Patrick Phillips, p. 71; Fred Sacksteder, p. 102; Bennett Tillison, p. 54; Larry Weiss, p. 39 top; John Wenck, p. 32 top; www.catskillmarket.com, p. 106 right; www.ttaeventworks.com, p. 101 top.

All other photographs © 2002 Liz Steger

BY MARC HARTZMAN

FOUND ON eBAY

101 GENUINELY BIZARRE ITEMS FROM THE WORLD'S ONLINE YARD SALE

with photographs by *LIZ STEGER*

UNIVERSE

Dear Friends,

I always saved stuff growing up. Toys, tchotchkes, whatever. My room usually looked like it was attacked by a couple of wild hyenas. When it was visited by my father—who truly enjoyed throwing things out—I knew there would be trouble. "What do you need all this crap for? Clean up this room or I'm coming up with the garbage bag and I'll clean it myself!" he'd say. It struck fear into my heart every time. Fortunately, Mom would come to the rescue and straighten up the place. My stuff was saved. And today I'm sure it's all worth a fortune. Thanks to eBay, I can finally cash in.

One man's junk is truly another man's treasure. On eBay, anyone can become a bona fide seller of absolutely anything—whether it's childhood stuff, true collectibles, historical knickknacks, general mundane necessities, cars, real estate, or something found in the gutter. The world is your marketplace. That's the beauty of eBay. Just type in a keyword and chances are you'll find whatever you're looking for. Browse and you can easily find things you never knew existed. Or things you never would have imagined needing. It's all out there in a free-for-all capitalistic market gone awry. And schlock is a hot item.

People sell everything not only because they can, but because it's fun. Yet it's not like a garage sale where you just stick something outside on a table and hope some sucker hands over some cash for it. With eBay, selling takes a bit more effort and finesse. You've got to photograph the item, write a catchy, informative description, and fill out the sale forms. Plus there's a meager fee. For some unique items it's well worth it. But what about a true piece of junk? Is it really a "conversation piece"? Perhaps it's worth listing just to see if someone will bite. And then there's the excitement of checking your auctions, hoping that the bidding keeps rising and rising until you've suddenly made a small fortune on what you thought was a worthless piece of crap. Imagine the thrill of getting paid for your old Speedo.

On the other hand, eBay builds little communities online in the way brick-and-mortar stores cannot. What better place to find other people who like the strange things that you do? Where else can you find a group of people who collect cans of rattlesnake meat? Enthusiasts of taxidermied frog musicians? Or a couple of people who would engage in a bidding war over your wisdom teeth? Small informal clubs of buyers and sellers sprout up based around shared hobbies and pastimes.

But what makes people decide to part with a vintage French enema pump or a two-headed calf? And where do they get this stuff? Fortunately, eBay allows you to ask sellers questions. I took advantage of that opportunity to find out a little more about these bizarre auctions. At the same time, I figured I'd match their unusual nature. Would someone selling something weird even notice when I was being weird? Usually not. They were too concerned with providing answers to the best of their knowledge and making a sale. Yes, the American entrepreneurial spirit is alive and well. Just slightly twisted.

Someday my kid will have a messy room filled with silly junk that needs to go. And I'll end up in the dreaded position of sounding just like my father, "What do you need all this crap for? Clean up your room!" Then we'll get online and make some money.

—Marc Hartzman

FEATURED ITEMS:

SEARCH

GREAT GIFT IDEAS:

	BIRTHDAYS
72	Eel Skins
49	Gallon of Texas Well Water
32	Can of Rattlesnake Meat
88	Pretty Plunger
89	Moose Poop
42	Men's Speedo like Swimsuit
08	NJ Turnpike Tumbler and Pennant
80	My Big Toenail
45	Seattle Earthquake Bill
39	Belt Buckle with Glass Eye
54	Pile of Dug Relics
107	Fish Carved from Fungus
89	Fossil Dinosaur Poop
100	1972 Gremlin

	HOLIDAYS
80	Mike's Wart
106	Firewood
37	Natural Emu Egg
79	Abe Lincoln Hair
78	Wisdom Teeth
12	Western Back Scratcher
16	Beer Cap Man
50	Coins of the Dead
09	60s Racetrack Menu
25	Britney Spears Portrait

94	A Penis-Shaped Cheeto
26	Scotch Tape Dispenser
55	Weird Old Photo—Spooky

	APOLOGIES
48	Lot of 4 Wintario Lottery Tickets
55	Lucky 1895 Book with 4 Leaf Clovers
86	19th-Century Enema Machine
73	Human Femur Bone
95	Medical Castration Tool
73	Mummified Possum!
62	Preserved Shark Fetus
95	Bed Pan Urinal Combo
72	Freak Sideshow Gaff
106	1 Wooden Leg
95	Civil War Catheter

	JUST BECAUSE
21	Truck Driver's Prayer Poem
38	Goat Toenail Bracelet
33	Old Package of Beech-Nut Gum
73	Skunk Skull
79	Antique Human Hair
49	Mississippi Flood Water
55	1929 Iowa High School Diploma
81	My Colon
12	Ear-Wax Stick
94	Potted Penis Plants

Item #1000259432

OLD LARD BUCKET

Category: **Collectibles:Housewares & Kitchenware**

Location......... **Comanche, TX**	Seller Rating.....................**113**
# of Bids.....................**6**	Selling Price.........**$5.50**

DESCRIPTION:

This is just an old rusty Swift's Pure Lard bucket. Almost 5"
tall and pretty rusty. I think it is just a rusty old bucket, but
my wife insisted that I put it on here since it is soooo old. Well
anyway, here it is. Happy bidding!

QUESTION FOR SELLER:

> Could the bucket be turned over and be used as a small drum?
> I often like to take classic rock and interpret it on old buckets—if
> they're empty. In the past I've wowed folks with
> covers of Debbie Gibson, Bachman Turner Overdrive,
> and GWAR. It keeps me busy.

I suppose you could turn it over and use it for a drum.
Thanks for your questions. If you have any more, just
drop me another email.

click for larger photo

Conversation Piece!

Item # 1153931543

DUNCAN MILLER 5CENT 10CENT PARKING METER LAMP

Category: Collectibles:Coin-Op, Banks & Casino: Other Coin-Op

Made from an actual parking meter. Still works too! It makes a really neat timer. And there's no lock, so you can get your money out.

Location . . . . **Owensboro, KY**
Starting Bid **$9.00**
# of Bids 5
Selling Price **$31.77**

Item # 1163144511

VINTAGE NJ TURNPIKE TUMBLER + PENNANT

Category: Collectibles:Transportation:Maps, Atlases: Road Maps:US

Felt pennant, small size. Glass shows a map of the turnpike and says, "118 miles of effortless driving."

Location . . . . **New York**
Starting Bid **$7.50**
# of Bids 3
Selling Price **$10.76**

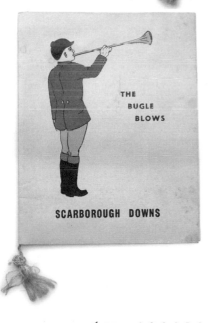

Item # 1154933654

SCARBOROUGH DOWNS RACETRACK MENU, 60s

Category: Everything Else:Equestrian Equipment:Racing:General

A little dirty and lots of notes written inside, but still a fun piece. Great find.

Location . . . . **Kansas City**
Starting Bid **$2.00**
# of Bids 5
Selling Price **$16.53**

GREASE-STAINED!

Item #5798664223

OLD BOX OF CRAYONS

Category: **Toys & Hobbies:Vintage:General**

Location.................................**WA**	# of Bids..............................**0**
Starting Bid.....................**$1.99**	Selling Price..........**No Sale**

DESCRIPTION:

Not sure on an age, but it says Crayola only made fifty colors. Top flap is gone, and there's some pencil on the front. But this would still be a great display piece for its era. There are some of the original crayons inside too!

✉ QUESTION FOR SELLER:

> I've always been a fan of colors. You mentioned there were fifty,
> but it says only six. Of course, that's all you need. I'm fed up with
> the fancy new colors. I think blue is best. Thanks.

There's yellow, red, green, and black inside. It says on the side of the box that they made only fifty colors, which I mentioned for dating purposes only. This cute little box did originally have 6. I always thought these would make a neat display on an old school desk.

click for larger photo

Item #1000286349

EAR-WAX STICK THING!!

Category: Everything Else:Weird Stuff: Totally Bizarre

EAR-WAX REMOVERS. YEP! That's what these are. Purchased while on a trip to Kyoto, Japan. I thought they were swizzle sticks! Successful bidder may purchase additional at same price! I have eight. PLEASE NOTE: YOU ARE BIDDING ON ONE ONLY! Bamboo topped with papier-mâché figure of Japanese child. About 8 inches long.

Location	**PA**
Starting Bid	**$2.99**
# of Bids	**1**
Selling Price	**$2.99**

Item #1013735203

WESTERN BACK SCRATCHER

Category: Everything Else:Weird Stuff: Totally Bizarre

This is a great piece of Western history, made from an old cow rib bone. Finished up nice with a hanger. And you know what? The darn thing works great! Perfect Xmas present for that special buckaroo! No reserve!

Location	**South Dakota**
Starting Bid	**$9.99**
# of Bids	**1**
Selling Price	**$9.99**

Item #1604208730

LUCKY COWBOY BINGO DOLL

Category: **Toys & Hobbies:Games:General**

Location...	**Central New York**	# of Bids	**1**
Starting Bid	**$2.50**	Selling Price	**$2.50**

SPIFFY!

1963 J. F. KENNEDY GARDEN GNOME

Category: **Collectibles:Historical Memorabilia:President:1900–1975**

Location	**Central Maine**	# of Bids	**8**
Starting Bid	**$35.00**	Selling Price	**$103.50**

DESCRIPTION:

In 1963 the German garden gnome manufacturer Heissner created an entirely new type of garden gnomes—politicians. A set of four was offered—Khrushchev of Russia, Adenauer of Germany, de Gaulle of France, and JFK. At this time they were no success— a real flop. Only a few were manufactured and sold. That's the reason why this is a unique offer at eBay—these garden gnomes are extremely rare. JFK is about 10" tall, made of earthenware, and hand-painted. The last owner repainted parts of the shirt, the trousers, and the shoes. There are some paint rubs, a small loss of paint, and a chip missing on the left shoe—see our images. Otherwise JFK is in excellent condition. You will scarcely find another one.

click for larger photo

Lift can for BIG surprise!

PARTY FUN!

Item #1470683814

**BEER CAP MAN
FOLK ART**

Category: Collectibles:Houcewaree & Kitchenware:Barware

A truly great piece of folk art from the past. A bottle cap man made with a Genesee beer can body, Genesee beer cap arms and legs, thumb tack eyes and nose, with a plastic ashtray on top. This is definitely a man since the body is anatomically correct—you lift the can and his penis falls down. It is 10 3/4" high, the front of the can has some very minor scratching, and the back has a couple of small rust spots.

Location	**Upstate NY**
Starting Bid	**$9.99**
# of Bids	2
Selling Price	**$12.50**

DOG REPELLENT FROM 1933

Category: **Collectibles:Science, Medical**

Location.... **Youngstown, OH**	# of Bids..................................1
Starting Bid............ **$9.49**	Selling Price.......... **$9.49**

DESCRIPTION:

This unusual product, DOGZOFF, is a 6" high, clear glass, empty bottle. Some dark product stain. Dated 1933. "Discourages dogs. Keeps them away from plants, shrubs, trees, walls, tires." 6 fluid oz. Bohlender Plant Chemicals, Inc., Tipp City, Ohio.

✉ **QUESTION FOR SELLER:**

> Hello. Is this here something I can put on my leg
> to keep the neighbor's dog off? He's cute and all,
> but I don't go that way. Thank you!

This product is older and likely is for DISPLAY or AMUSE-MENT purposes only. Thanks for the inquiry!

click for larger photo

GOD BLESS OUR MOBILE HOME TRIVET

Category: **Collectibles:Housewares & Kitchenware:Trivets**

Location............**Lakeland, FL**	# of Bids...............................2
Starting Bid................**$6.50**	Selling Price............**$7.00**

TRUCK DRIVER'S PRAYER

Dear God above
bless this truck I drive
And help me keep someone alive
Be my mortal sight this day
On streets where little children play

Bless my helper fast asleep
When the night is long and deep
And keep my cargo safe and sound
Through the hours big and round

Make my judgement sound as steel
And be my hands upon the wheel
Bless the traveler going past
And teach him not to go so fast

Give me the strength for every trip
So I may care for what they ship
And make me mindful every mile
That life is just a little while

"BIG MARC"

Item #5924248630

TRUCK DRIVER'S PRAYER POEM

Category: Everything Else

Starting Bid	$3.99
Quantity	2
# of Bids	2
Selling Price	$5.00

Classy!

1960 BOWLING TROPHY

Category: **Sports:Memorabilia:Bowling**

Location	**Minnesota**	# of Bids	**5**
Starting Bid	**$4.99**	Selling Price	**$16.50**

DESCRIPTION:

You are bidding on a bowling trophy from 1960. Says "Town Club League Champions 1960." 7 1/2" high and 7" wide.

✉ QUESTION FOR SELLER:

> This is a real dandy. My mother stinks at bowling. She bowls a 70
> and her friends make fun of her. Could I replace the plaque and
> pass this off as her own? That would shut those old
> bags up.

What a great idea! The plaque could be replaced. Actually, how long has she been bowling? Maybe you could just add her name to it. Only problem, the bowler appears to be male. Best of luck.

click for larger photo

OPRAH SIGNED BASEBALL!

Category: **Sports:Autographs:Baseball:General**

Location.............**New York**	# of Bids.............................**0**
Starting Bid..............**$9.99**	Selling Price......**NO SALE**

DESCRIPTION:

That's right, this is a baseball signed by Oprah. Just a printing of her signature, of course. This is a rare promotional item sent to a select few for her Oprah magazine launch. Why she sent out a baseball I don't know, but it's pretty neat! What a bizarre thing to have in your collection! Great conversation piece.

Item # 1440316227

BRITNEY SPEARS PORTRAIT

Category: Collectibles:Art:Prints:Portraits

Pencil drawing of pop's reigning princess. Frameable.

Location .... **Glenn Dale**
Starting Bid **$10.00**
# of Bids 1
Selling Price $10.00

STUNNING LIKENESS!

Item #1143331859

GRANDMA'S OLD QUILTING SQUARES AND SCRAPS

Category: Collectibles:Housewares & Kitchenware:Textiles:Quilts

You are bidding on the leftovers in Grandma's old quilt box. Lots of good old scraps for mending quilts or starting a new one! Please ask all questions before you bid! All items are sold as is.

Location .... **Sharon, Tennessee**
Starting bid **$9.99**
# of Bids 1
Selling Price **$9.99**

> Is there a moth ball stink to any of these? (No offense, but I've encoun-
> tered this horrid type of problem in the past and wound up in court for
> six months.) Was your grandmother famous? Like that lovely Bea Arthur?
> That would make these extra special. Thank you.

I didn't notice any odor before, and I went back and checked again. No, my grandmother wasn't famous, except to me and I loved her dearly. But if these quilt squares had belonged to her I wouldn't be selling them.

Item #1150813963

UNIQUE SCOTCH TAPE DISPENSER

Category: Business, Office & Industrial:Desk Accessories

You are bidding on a unique Scotch tape dispenser. It has a knight in armor riding on a horse in its armor. It is black with a gold color overlay on the front. On the back was stamped "W. Germany." It is in good condition.

Location .... **Sedalia, MO**
Starting Bid **$6.00**
# of Bids 0
Selling Price .... **No Sale**

BAGS OF REAL SHREDDED MONEY!

Category: **Collectibles:Autographs, Paper & Writing:Paper**

Location	**Brookfield, OH**	# of Bids	3
Starting Bid	**$1.00**	Selling Price	**$3.00**

1970s LIQUID PAPER WETNAP

Category: **Collectibles:Everything Else:Health & Wellness**

Location	**Raleigh, NC**	# of Bids	1
Starting Bid	$9.95	Selling Price	**$9.95**

DESCRIPTION:

This is an unopened "Off-hand" cleaning towel made by Liquid Paper Corporation in 1979 (copyright date is on the back of the package)! Yes, it's a 22-year-old wetnap! And though I have only a handful (pun intended) of these, I sacrificed one and opened it to enjoy a towel that was STILL moist—and still had a strong citrus smell, one that was reminiscent of wetnaps I smelled in the 1970s! There is no guarantee, but my guess is that this hand towel is still fresh and ready to go! You need this vintage hand

towel for your collection! Own a piece of hand-cleaning-towel history!

click for larger photo

front view

Off-hand ®
Hand Cleaning Towel

back view

Off-hand Hand Cleaning Towel

© 1979 LIQUID PAPER CORPORATION
Box 61 Boston MA 02199

Made in USA

2

Item #1000266887

RARE PICKLE!

Category: **Everything Else:Weird Stuff:Slightly Unusual**

Location **Alexandria, VA**	# of Bids...................1
Starting Bid **$1.00**	Selling Price **No Sale**

DESCRIPTION:

This is the LAST pickle from the pickle jar. What are the chances? Most would believe that I would eat it, but no. This is the first time I have sold it instead of eating it, and that makes it rare and a collector's item. I will even make a certificate of authenticity.

✉ **QUESTION FOR SELLER:**

> Hello! One time when I was younger I ate the last pickle and my
> sister got very upset. She punched me square in the face. Years
> later I spiked her soda with pickle juice as a meager
> revenge. Ever since, the last pickle has been special
> and dear to me. Is this pickle kosher? Thank you
> for your help in this matter.

Yes, I think it's kosher. Well, they took my pickle item
down anyway. Check out www.drivenbyboredom.com

click for larger photo

Tastes like chicken!

Item #1000280775

1949 CAN OF RATTLESNAKE MEAT

Category: Collectibles:Animals:Reptile, Amphibian:Snake

This is an original can of Ross Allen's Genuine Diamondback Rattlesnake w/Supreme Sauce. This can measures 3 inches tall and the diameter is 2.25 inches. It is in great shape and has never been opened. There is some rust and dust on the top. Where are you going to find something like this except on eBay? Buy your souvenir can today. This is the only one I have. I bought it at an estate auction. This would be a great gift for the macho man, Ross Allen fan! The can is dated 1949. Thanks for looking and please email any questions you may have.

Location . . . . **Iowa**
Starting Bid **$9.99**
# of Bids **14**
Selling Price **$40.51**

Item #1150072707

PAIR OF HOLMES SARDINES CANS

Category: Collectibles:Advertising:Food & Restaurant:Other Items

These two 15 oz. Holmes Sardines cans are in rough condition with some rusting, dents, and paint loss. They would make for good conversation pieces!

Location . . . . **Littleton, CO**
Starting Bid **$1.99**
# of Bids **1**
Selling Price **$1.99**

Item #1150999068

VINTAGE QUAKER QUICK GRITS BOX & QUAKER MUG

Category: Collectibles:Advertising:Food & Restaurant:Cereal:Quaker

Old grits box. Just cleaning things out. Comes with a collectible mug.

Location . . . . **Central California**
Starting Bid **$5.00**
# of Bids 1
Selling Price $5.00

Item #5559085054

OLD PACKAGE OF BEECH-NUT GUM

Category: Advertising:Candy:General

This is a nice old 5-stick package of Beech-Nut Gum. It has been displayed in a shadow box while in my possession for the last fifteen years. Bid with confidence, as I offer a return privilege if you are not completely satisfied.

Location . . . . **Wisconsin**
Starting Bid **$9.99**
# of Bids 2
Selling Price $10.50

Item #1000268749

CORNED BEEF

Category: **Home & Garden:Food & Beverage:Meat, Poultry & Seafood**

Location............ **Los Angeles**	# of Bids...........................6
Starting Bid............. **$1.00**	Selling Price........... **$5.50**

DESCRIPTION.

Think of all you can do with this versatile product! Put it in your bomb shelter! Make a lamp out of it! Fling it from your car at high speeds!

✉ QUESTION FOR SELLER:

> My grandmother collects canned meats and I thought this would
> be a nice addition. She dusts them every Sunday and occasionally
> on Wednesdays if the week is especially dusty. Is it
> easy to open? I prefer not, that would deter her
> from ever eating it.

It doesn't seem easy to open. In fact, it requires a key, which may prove too much for Grandma's arthritic, brittle fingers.

click for larger photo

SIAMESE TWIN M&M CANDY

Category: **Collectibles:Advertising:Candy & Nuts:M&M/Mars**

Location......**Charleston, WV**	# of Bids.......................1
Starting Bid.............**$1.00**	Selling Price...........**$1.00**

Item #1000285154

PEACH SEED MONKEY

**Category: Everything Else:Weird Stuff:
Slightly Unusual**

Monkey is hand carved out of a peach seed
and in excellent condition. I purchased part
of an estate and the monkey came along.
The lady told me the monkey was carved in
a foxhole during WWII by her grandfather.

Location .... **Oklahoma City**
Starting Bid **$3.99**
# of Bids 2
Selling Price $5.55

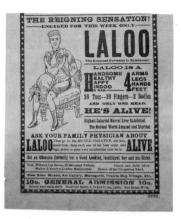

Item #8360220731

CARNIVAL FREAK SHOW AD

**Category: Collectibles:Historical
Memorabilia:Circus, Carnival**

Very old newspaper clipping (late 1800s) of
Laloo. He had a parasitic twin dangling from
his torso, which made him a very popular
attraction. You just don't see many folks like
that anymore. Great item.

Location .... **Canada**
Starting Bid **$9.99**
# of Bids 5
Selling Price $21.51

Item #2322001912

REAL NATURAL EMU EGG

**Category: Home & Garden:Home
Furnishings:General**

Beautiful emu egg. About $5^1/_2$" long, $10^1/_2$"
around. Hollowed out.

Location .... **Heartland USA**
Starting Bid **$3.00**
# of Bids 5
Selling Price $10.08

Item #1648224189

GOAT TOENAIL BRACELET

Category: Everything Else:Weird Stuff: Totally Bizarre

I bought two of these bracelets from a company that sells strange objects from other countries. The bracelets supposedly came from Guatemala. I sold the first one on eBay about three years ago to a woman doctor from the east coast. It was about two weeks before Christmas. Shortly after New Year's this doctor emailed wanting to know the origin of the bracelet. It seems her hospital had a big Christmas party for a group of Latin American children who were sponsored for treatments there. This bracelet was a gift from her to a little girl from Guatemala. Well, when the little girl opened her present, she started screaming hysterically and ran from the room. She would not tell the doctor about the significance of the bracelet. I emailed the company, started calling, and all I got was a runaround. I never did find out why the little girl was so traumatized. This bracelet is clean and well made with a beautiful textile for the band. Each "toenail" is hand sewn. Makes the most eerie sound when shaken. I figure these were worn around the wrists and ankles.

Demonic?

Location	**SD**
Starting Bid	**$9.99**
# of Bids	0
Selling Price	**No Sale**

Item #1000255584

BELT BUCKLE WITH GLASS EYE

Category: Clothing & Accessories:
Men: Accessories

If you ever wanted a third eye so you can
be a cyclops, this item is for you!! Be differ-
ent and have that third eye at the center of
your leather belt buckle. This blue glass
eye stares at the viewer and looks remark-
ably real. Belt buckle is 3 1/4 inches wide
and in excellent condition.

Location	**Naperville, IL**
Starting Bid	**$24.99**
# of Bids	1
Selling Price	$24.99

Item #5524522603

MEN'S USED CARGO PANTS

Category: Clothing & Accessories: Mens Clothing: General

Approximately 31" to 32" waist, 30" inseam length. All cotton and
heavy duty. Two back pockets, two side pockets, two leg pockets
all with button flaps. Drab olive green in color. The fit on these is
excellent (more flattering than the standard army pant). Great with
a pair of boots! They are used and have some repairs: major repairs
across the left leg pocket and left rear pocket; small repair on front of
left leg pocket. These repairs only add to their rugged look (and I've
done my best to picture these).

Location	**Houston, TX**
Starting Bid	**$6.99**
# of Bids	0
Selling Price	No Sale

📷 Item #1604254090

DUCT TAPE NECKTIE

Category: **Clothing & Accessories:Mens Accessories:Ties**

Location...... **McPherson, KS**
Starting Bid.................**$5.00**

# of Bids.................................**3**
Selling Price.............**$8.50**

DESCRIPTION:

This is a fabulous duct tape necktie. This tie measures 59 inches long and ties into a standard knot very easily. I have made several of these ties, but this is my first one on eBay. It is made out of 100% duct tape. This tie is a great way to stand out.

✉ QUESTION FOR SELLER:

> Fancy lookin' tie there. Is it an original design? Have you worn it
> around, and if so, did you get any compliments? I'm not much
>> of a trendsetter, but I've always wanted to be.

click for larger photo

I took the measurements off one of my dad's ties. I have not worn my duct tape ties around too much, but I do wear my duct tape wallet all the time. Presently I am working on making a complete suit, which I intend to wear to prom in a few years.

Chic!

Item # 1630908614

MEN'S SPEEDO-LIKE SWIMSUIT

**Category: Clothing & Accessories:Men:
Clothing:Swimwear**

Yellow & Black Men's Speedo-Like
Swimsuit. This is a used but clean men's
Speedo-like swimsuit, size large. I'm selling
off all of my "vintage" swimsuits that I used
to wear (when I was younger and had a
body) in the 90s. I will be putting them on
eBay over the next several weeks. Thanks
for looking and keep cool.

Location .... **New York**
Starting Bid **$4.00**
# of Bids **12**
Selling Price **$20.50**

Item #1156227138

VINTAGE SEARS SALES
PATRIOTIC SALES HAT

**Category: Collectibles:Advertising:Retail
Establishments:Department Store**

Boy, you just don't see these anymore.
This must've been worn by a spirited Sears
salesman at a big sale. Great shape.
Still wearable.

Location .... **New Orleans**
Starting Bid **$8.88**
# of Bids **1**
Selling Price **$8.88**

Item #1601038615

COLORADO STATE
PENITENTIARY BELT BUCKLE

**Category: Clothing & Accessories:Mens
Accessories:Belts**

Metal belt buckle from Canon City, CO.

Location .... **Southwest Missouri**
Starting Bid **$4.99**
# of Bids **1**
Selling Price **$4.99**

ONE USED SIZE-9 WORK BOOT

Category: **Clothing & Accessories:Men:Footwear**

Location **Dallas, Oregon**	# of Bids 2
Starting Bid **$1.00**	Selling Price **$1.25**

DESCRIPTION:

That's right, one worn-out work boot. Somebody stole the left boot so I must sell the right boot. Now you might laugh, but realize that this boot being almost two years old has seen many places including but not limited to: Seattle Washington, most of the state of Oregon, northern Calif., the Polk County and Marion County jails, all three of my kids' asses, the underside of my atv's rear tire on accident!!, most of the wiggler bars in the Pacific Northwest, and last but not least the underside of my bed. Whoever stole my left boot here is your chance to get the other one. Or if you only have a right leg this is a real bargain. If you can get it to talk to you, you'll laugh your ass off.

click for larger photo

ANTIQUE LEATHER WALLET

Category: **Antiques:Other Antiques**

Location...................**Colorado**
Starting Bid.................**$24.95**

# of Bids...................................**5**
Selling Price.........**$35.78**

DESCRIPTION:

This old wallet has fox and hound scenes on it. There's a notebook inside with a note. It says, "This book of Levi Ballards was bought at Redfield, Iowa in 1853 Sept. when the old house was bought. Paid $100 for 80 acres. Sold to Will Kenworthy for $40 per acre in 1876." A fun gift for collectors or anyone named Will Kenworthy.

click for larger photo

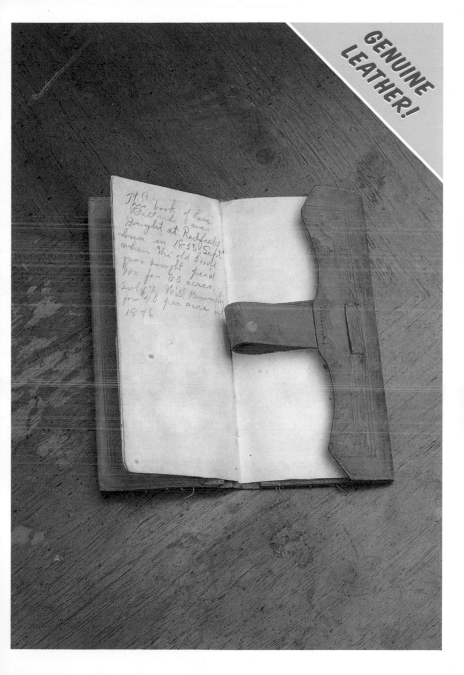

GENUINE LEATHER!

#1 front view *#1 back view* *#2 front view* *#2 back view*

#3 front view *#3 back view* *#4 front view* *#4 back view*

Item #1660487889

LOT OF 4 OLD WINTARIO LOTTERY TICKETS

Category: Collectibles:Autographs, Paper & Writing:Paper

Not a winner in the bunch. But still a fun memento of 1970s gambling.

Location . . . . **Canada**
Starting Bid **$2.99**
# of Bids **1**
Selling Price **$2.99**

Item #1135296053

1 GALLON OF GENUINE TEXAS WELL WATER

Category: Everything Else

Here is something interesting. For sale—1 gallon of genuine Canyon, Texas, well water. Is it better than Evian? Could be. PERRIER? Maybe. Great for making coffee on Monday morning. Water to be sent in a gallon container anywhere in the continental United States. Shipping free.

Location . . . . **Canyon, TX**
Starting Bid **$12.49**
# of Bids **0**
Selling Price . . . . **No Sale**

Item #1000299215

2001 MUDDY MISSISSIPPI FLOOD WATER BY THE JAR

Category: Collectibles:Historical Memorabilia:Other Historical Memorabilia

This is flood water taken from what is the second-highest flood on the Mississippi in Wisconsin. I know 'cause it's in my yard and basement and still coming. Would make a great gift for the person who has everything. Approx. 12 ounces. Will take from basement or the yard.

Location . . . . **WI**
Starting Bid **$2.00**
# of Bids **0**
Selling Price . . . . **No Sale**

Item #1118688722

SEATTLE 6.8 EARTHQUAKE DIRT!

Category: Collectibles:Historical Memorabilia

Be the first on your block to own your own piece of a backyard in Issaquah (close to Seattle) that was tumbled around by the recent earthquake! You will receive a small bag of dirt from my backyard. Who knows, maybe if you pour it on your backyard, you might be able to grow your very own earthquake! As an extra bonus, the dirt will include some grass and weeds, also guaranteed to have survived the earthquake! Comes with a handwritten piece of paper stating this is authentic Issaquah earthquake-survived dirt.

Location . . . . **Issaquah, WA**
Starting Bid . . . . **$.01**
# of Bids **0**
Selling Price . . . . **No Sale**

Item #1000261485

COINS OF THE DEAD

**Category: Collectibles:Cultures &
Religions:Wiccan, Pagan**

I bought these years ago in a Clark's
auction. They were in a lot of about
sixty lead tokens excavated from a
first-century graveyard in Ostia, the
port of Rome. I later learned it was
Roman custom to place a coin in the
mouth of the deceased to pay the
ferryman on the Styx, the river that
separated the world of the living
from the underworld, and that lead
was the favored metal of Pluto, the
god of Hell—to him it was like gold.
So that's what these coins or tokens
are—"tickets to Hell," I guess you'd
have to say. I think I can see a ship
on the small one and what looks like
an angel on the large one. Lead is
such a soft metal, and when you
factor in its grisly provenance, the
flesh of the corpse around it eaten
away by worms and then even the
bones of the skull disintegrating, it's
amazing there's anything left at all.

Location . . . . **Eau Claire, WI**
Starting Bid . . . . **$.99**
# of Bids 5
Selling Price **$5.50**

Item #1000276525

FUNERAL EYE CAPS

Category: **Antiques:Science & Medicine**

Location	**NE Ohio**	# of Bids	**5**
Starting Bid	**$2.00**	Selling Price	**$10.50**

DESCRIPTION:

3 boxes of eye caps . . . looks like they are used to keep the eyes shut after embalming . . . good advertising boxes . . . Many funeral home/embalming items to be listed this week and next . . . check out all the auctions & bookmark this site . . . all the items will be at least twenty-five years old . . . many from the 30s/40s . . . email w/???

QUESTION FOR SELLER:

> Hello. Could these caps be comfortably worn over
> the eyes at night? I wonder if it would help me
> sleep. Blindfolds just don't do the trick.

These have sharp bumps all over them . . . I think they go directly on the eye and the bumps hold the eye lids closed . . . for good.

click for larger photo

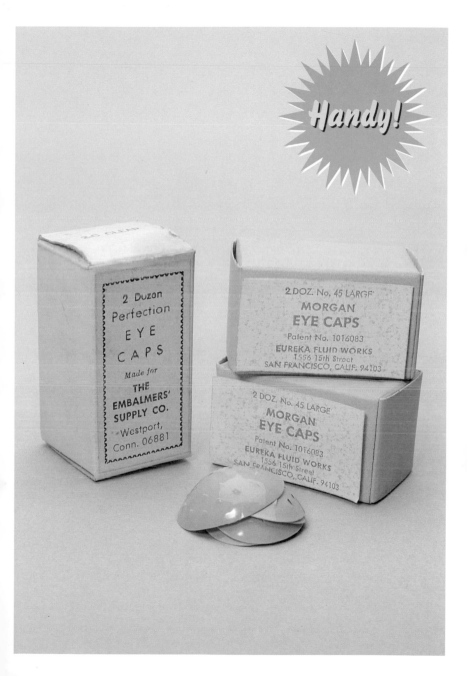

JUNK!

Item #1000307692

PILE OF DUG ARTIFACTS, RELICS, ETC.

Category: Everything Else

You are bidding on a pile of items that were excavated with the aid of a metal detector, dug from trash/bottle pits, or eyeballed. As-is condition. Glass, brass, lead, aluminum, etc. suitable for playing with, staring at, arts & crafts projects, still life, cherry picking. Comes in a zip-lock bag. Good luck & thanks for bidding!

Location	**SC**
Starting Bid	**$8.88**
# of Bids	**0**
Selling Price	**No Sale**

View 1

View 2

✉   **QUESTION FOR SELLER:**   ▲

> As an avid digger, I've found metal objects throughout the northern half
> of the United States. I once found a red Pinto buried in Montana. There
> were three bucks in the glove compartment! I'm wondering where these
> objects were found. I don't want to waste my time where the ground's
> already been dug.

You must be avid if you dug up a whole car! The objects were all found in
Florida, mostly Pensacola.

Item #1408821408

1929 IOWA DIPLOMA— HAMPTON HIGH

Category: Books:School Annuals

Old 1929 diploma from HAMPTON HIGH
SCHOOL. This is in as good a condition as
when it was presented. The student was
Edna Alice Arnett. If you're family, you might
want this. If you know of someone who
graduated from this school in that year, this
has all of their names on it. Hampton, Iowa.

Location . . . . **Nampa, Idaho**
Starting Bid **$7.00**
# of Bids 1
Selling Price **$7.00**

Item #1000303938

106-YEAR-OLD 4 LEAF CLOVERS IN 1895 BOOK

Category: Everything Else:Weird Stuff

These are three real four-leaf clovers that
I found in a book of Coleridge's poems from
1895. Somebody picked them and pressed
them in this book over one hundred years
ago! This is a great book too. The book is
entitled *The Poetical Works of Samuel Taylor
Coleridge*. It has the Kubla Khan Xanadu
poem in it and other nice poetry. The book
is in very good condition.

Location . . . . **Eugene, Oregon**
Starting Bid **$9.50**
# of Bids 8
Selling Price **$31.50**

Item #1658669743

WEIRD OLD PHOTO—SPOOKY

Category: Collectibles:Art & Photo Images

This photo scares the bejeezus outta me.
Frame at your own risk.

Location . . . . **Pennsylvania**
Starting Bid **$1.00**
# of Bids 1
Selling Price **$1.00**

Creepy!

ANTIQUE DOLL GRAVEYARD

Category: **Dolls & Bears:Dolls:Antique:Other Antique Dolls**

Location.................................**SC**	# of Bids...................................**12**
Starting Bid **$49.49**	Selling Price **$160.00**

DESCRIPTION:

You are bidding on a doll/figurine "graveyard." All of the pieces were dug while searching for antique bottles over the years. Most of the items are turn-of-the-century & have been washed with a toothbrush, using very little elbow grease. Approximately thirty of the arms and legs are undamaged, & there are marked pieces included. The others are all damaged & incomplete (except for a couple of small head & shoulders). Quite a variety, and lots of it! The pile measures approximately 11" x 20" as shown in the first photo. Bisque, ceramic, porcelain. This stuff is just begging to be framed and stared at for hours on end. Sorta reminds me of a very bizarre coral reef! I'm almost ready to run out and buy an aquarium!

click for larger photo

The winner of the auction on eBay with the #_____ will recieve the entire human soul of Michael Dillion.

Signed in the presence of God, the Father:

Jordan Brock

(Jordan Brock - the current owner of the soul of Michael Dillion)

Item #1000303366

THE SOUL OF 1 HUMAN BEING

Category: **Everything Else: Metaphysical**

Location	**Kentucky**	# of Bids	**3**
Starting Bid	**$.01**	Selling Price	**$ 71**

DESCRIPTION:

Wouldn't it be nice to have more than just one soul? Perhaps you have previously lost or sold your soul? THIS IS YOUR LUCKY CHANCE!!! This is an auction for one soul of one of my friends. He, being an atheist, bet his soul that a friend of mine would beat another friend of mine in a game of Golden Eye on N64. Too bad for him, he lost and now his soul is mine, BUT NOW IT CAN BE YOURS!!! The winner of this auction will receive this signed certificate of confirmation (in ink). Please, no fake bidders. This is a serious auction. If you have any questions, feel free to email me.

click for larger photo

CLOSED BY EBAY

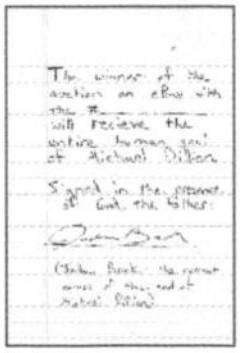

CUSTOM MADE!

detail

VAMPIRE KILLING SET!

Category: **Everything Else**

Location............	**New England**	# of Bids............................	2
Starting Bid	**$6.00**	Selling Price	**$7.50**

DESCRIPTION:

Just the thing to ward off Dracula. This set consists of a stake, mallet, and holy water bottle. The stake is 11½ inches long and is hand carved from solid oak. It has a wicked point, and a number of very unique decorative accents. There are four holes drilled through the stake to make it lighter, and there are three crosses burned between the holes. There is also a skull burned into the front near the top. The mallet is 13 inches long and is extremely sturdy and heavy. It features a custom handle, brass pommel, and a very sharp chrome spike on top. This set also comes with a genuine antique bottle to keep your holy water in. The wooden tools are constructed of the highest quality hardwoods and are very, very rugged and functional.

click for larger photo

UNBORN!

Item #3155831092
PRESERVED SHARK FETUS

Category: Collectibles:Animals:
Fish, Aquatic Mammals

The waters are safe—Jaws Jr. won't be going anywhere. This little fella moved from his mom right into this jar. (Don't worry, his mom was not hunted in order to preserve this fetus.) Great piece for your shelf.

Location . . . . **New York**
Starting Bid **$19.95**
# of Bids 6
Selling Price **$32.00**

SHARK

Item #1129471172
OLD STUFFED TOAD PLAYING A PIANO!!

Category: Collectibles:Animals:Reptile,
Amphibian:Frog

This is an old, stuffed, real frog playing a piano!!! (What, you've never seen a frog play a piano before???) I believe he is a bullfrog. He stands just a nose over $5\frac{1}{2}$ inches tall. His piano measures just over 6 inches tall and almost 5 inches wide. This bizarre little guy is quite a conversation piece. If you are nice to him he will take requests. When he goes on his musical tour his stage name is Frog Legs on the Ivories. He is looking for a family that likes maintenance-free pets as well as piano music. Maybe you can find a tiny brandy snifter to put on his piano for tips. Don't let him get away. You might not see another talented amphibian like him for a long, long time. (Is that a bad thing?)

Location . . . . **Elgin, IL**
Starting Bid **$5.00**
# of Bids 14
Selling Price **$47.00**

📷 **Item #1000226988**

FROG COIN PURSE

Category: **Collectibles:Weird Stuff:Really Weird**

Location	**Atlanta, GA**	# of Bids	9
Starting Bid	**$7.50**	Selling Price	**$32.78**

DESCRIPTION:

Absolutely odd and bizarre. This is a coin purse made out of a frog. Where the delicious frog legs would be is a zipper. It feels stiffer than glove leather but is not hard. The little front paws feel stuffed and will move for instance without breaking off. My guess would be that it might hold half a roll of quarters but it would really be stuffed.

📷 **Item #1000278795**

BULLFROG PLAYING A GUITAR

Category: **Everything Else:General**

Location........... **Brooklyn, NY**	# of Bids................**5**
Starting Bid................**$4.99**	Selling Price........ **$27.66**

DESCRIPTION:

This is a real beauty. It is 7½" high. Don't miss this one. They do not pop up every day.

✉ **QUESTION FOR SELLER:**

> Could you explain the process of mummifying a frog? I assume you
> made this baby yourself. I have a lot of ideas I'd like to incorpor-

click for larger photo

> ate with mummification. For instance: frogs playing
> ukuleles, frogs playing basketball, and maybe cross-
> dressing frogs. Other amphibians might be fun too.

I wish I knew how to do it. All I know is it's a real frog, I picked it up about ten years ago, and it never rotted. Somebody did a good job.

Dead!

🔲 Item #1000275179

REAL KILLER MOUSE

Category: **Home & Garden:Home Furnishings:Furnishings:General**

Location.. **Mouse Infested TX**
Starting Bid.............**$3.99**

# of Bids.................................**1**
Selling Price............**$3.99**

DESCRIPTION:

A preserved and dried real wild mouse. Just what you need. No one else on the block will have one. Has his little feet and tail. Grey fur. Get it for your cat.

✉ QUESTION FOR SELLER:

> Well stick a fork up my nose! This is neat. Did you catch the little
> stinker? I don't have a cat because they make me sneeze and their

> hair gets all over the damn place. But I'm wondering
> if this would make a fun play toy for my gerbil. Also,
> I have a young nephew who enjoys toys and such.

I didn't catch it. Came in a lot of freezer items I bought from a pet supplier. They are used to feed snakes and large lizards. Glad you like it.

click for larger photo

📷 Item #1000279479

HORNETS' NEST

Category: **Collectibles:Animals:Insect:Bee**

Location............ **Smithville, IN**   # of Bids.............................5
Starting Bid................**$1.00**   Selling Price.............**$2.25**

DESCRIPTION:

**Very big hornets' nest, 22" by 1 foot, in good shape. HORNETS
NOT INCLUDED.**

✉ QUESTION FOR SELLER:

> Would hornets be attracted to this and seek shelter inside? Or
> can it be stuffed with candy and be made into a pinata? I do
> oddball children's parties. Thank you very much.

No, the hornets would not be attracted to the nest. It
would make a great pinata. I never thought of that.
It has some beautiful pink and blue colors around it.
But it would be perfectly safe.

click for larger photo

ADORABLE!

TWO-HEADED CALF

Category: **Collectibles:Animals:Farm:Cow**

Location...................**Duck, WV**
Starting Bid.......**$20,000.00**

# of Bids...................................**0**
Selling Price..........**No Sale**

DESCRIPTION:

This antique oddity has been in my family tucked away in the closet since 1955 shortly after its birth. Two perfect heads, one complete body, full body mount, preserved in a glass case. Excellent condition. Authenticity verifiable.

QUESTION FOR SELLER:

> Howdy! Was this born on your farm? If so, how did the mother
> react? Did it ever travel with a sideshow? I couldn't imagine
> having another head, maybe another hand though.

click for larger photo

Yes, it was born on a farm in a small town in Virginia. The calf had one of its necks broken at birth (accidentally). This was not a farm in my family. My father apparently was attempting to collect a bill and took the animal in trade. From there he had it mounted.

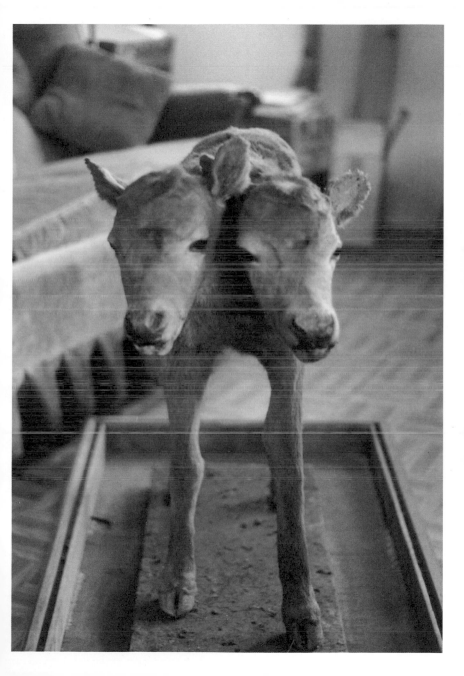

WHAT IS IT?

Item #1671096138
FREAK SIDESHOW GAFF

Category: Everything Else:Weird Stuff: Totally Bizarre

This ladies and gentlemen is legendary sideshow gaff builder Mark Frierson's newest creation—simply called a "What Is It?". And that is exactly what you will be asking yourselves, folks, when you gaze down, in amazement and wonder, into its devilishly beady black eyes! Is it a freak of nature? Man-made monstrosity? Or simply a government experiment gone awry? You decide! This strange and wonderful pocket-sized pal measures a demure 4 1/2" tall x 4" over all, including the base. This oddball little creature is made up of the body of a duckling, the head of a perch, fish fins for wings, a monkey's tail, and a horn on its nose.

Location . . . . **Houston, Texas**
Starting Bid **$75.00**
# of Bids 4
Selling Price **$92.50**

Item #1000273998
GENUINE COLORFUL EEL SKINS

Category: Collectibles:Animals:Fish, Aquatic Mammals

These hides are from some type of large eel. They are between 24 and 34 inches, and some are red and others are brown. All of them are leopard patterned, and you can use them to make wallets, purses, clothing, shoes, etc. You can also use them as wall decorations or just as unusual conversation pieces. I was told that the man who owned these (he passed away) WHOLESALED them for $35 apiece. I am starting the bidding at only $3 each with NO RESERVE!

Location . . . . **MSU Spartan Country**
Quantity 6
Starting Bid **$3.00**
# of Bids 2
Selling Price **$3.02**

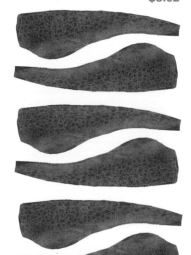

Item #1000227605

SKUNK SKULL

Category: Collectibles:Weird Stuff:Really Weird

THIS IS A NICE SKUNK SKULL, VERY CLEAN, NO CRACKS, ALL TEETH INTACT. TEACHERS: Get this for the classroom—great teaching tool!! I stand behind my product!! THANKS!!

Location .... **Skullshop—Idaho**
Starting Bid **$9.99**
# of Bids 1
Selling Price **$9.99**

Item #1000204487

MUMMIFIED POSSUM?

Category: Everything Else

I think this was a possum. It measures about 16 inches long without the tail. It was found while cleaning out a garage. It is really much more disgusting than the photos can show. It is half gone but the remains seem to be mummified. I thought it might be used for display or to send to someone you don't like! Buyer agrees not to hold seller responsible for any diseases or any other damages that could result from handling dead animals. It will be sent well wrapped in plastic & in a box.

Location .... **Long Island, New York**
Starting Bid **$1.50**
# of Bids 14
Selling Price **$103.50**

Item #3402453253

HUMAN FEMUR BONE

Category: Everything Else:Educational:General

Yes, this is a real human femur (thigh bone). It comes from a skeleton once used as an educational tool at my college. There is some damage at the upper and lower joint areas as there were once pins through these areas to attach the bone to the rest of the skeleton. It is about 15 1/2 inches long. Sold as is.

Location .... **The South**
Starting Bid **$9.99**
# of Bids 18
Selling Price **$48.00**

📷 Item #1000365661

MANNEQUIN LEG!

Category: **Collectibles:Lamps:Lamp Repair, Refurbishing**

Location **Laurel, Delaware**	# of Bids 5
Starting Bid $19.99	Selling Price **$26.00**

DESCRIPTION:

Does have small holes in bottom of foot for wire. 35" tall, was cut off. Good used condition with scratches. Made of fiberglass.

✉ QUESTION FOR SELLER:

> Good afternoon. Could you please give me more detailed instruct-
> ions on how I could build a lamp from this leg? What was this leg
> used for? Are there other uses besides lamps? My nephew plays a
> lot of tee-ball and this might make him more popular with his
> friends. Thank you.

Don't know too much about it but I sure sell a lot of them for that reason. It is from an old movie—Christmas Story, I think. You would need all the parts. We do not have any other thing that goes with it. I have seen on eBay ones that were finished that went for $300.00. www.davessurplus.com

click for larger photo

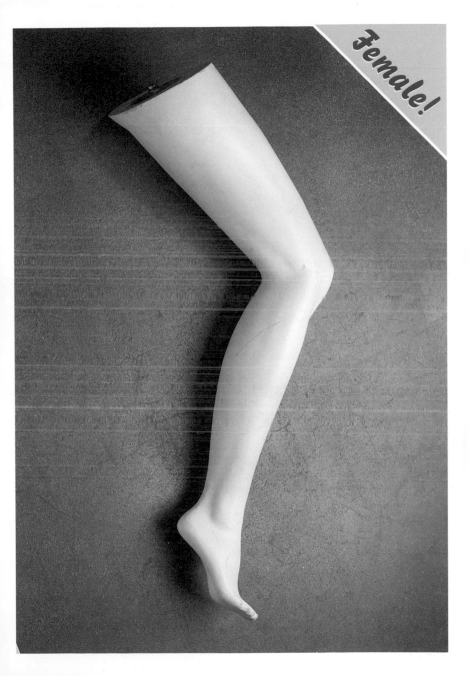

Female!

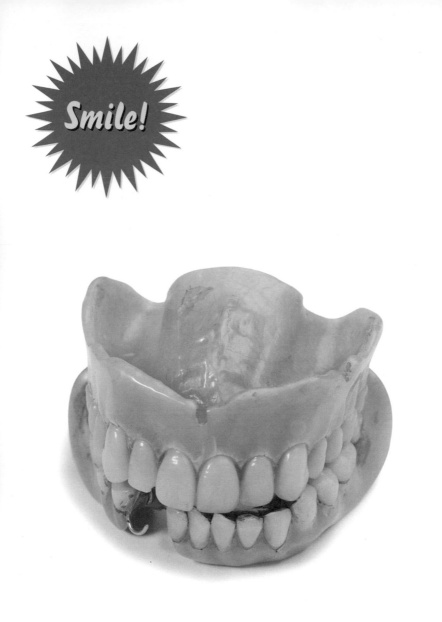

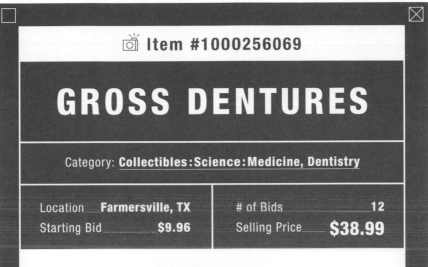

GROSS DENTURES

Category: **Collectibles:Science:Medicine, Dentistry**

Location...... **Farmersville, TX**

Starting Bid............... **$9.96**

# of Bids..................................... **12**

Selling Price........ **$38.99**

DESCRIPTION:

Thank you for shopping our dentures. These are 12 old dentures. Some have one or two teeth missing. Some only have a couple of teeth. They are in gross condition just like the old dentist took them back from his customer. These tools came out of an estate sale from a ninety-four-year-old dentist.

✉ **QUESTION FOR SELLER:**

> I recently lost a bunch of teeth in a gorilla show. No more corn on
> the cob for me. Have they been cleaned? I'm tired
> of this toothless crap.

If you think you want to use these just jump on it. Are they cleaned? You got to be crazy! I do not want to touch them much less clean them. They still have some of the corn on the cob on them.

click for larger photo

Item #1131930734

VINTAGE TOOTH SHADE MATCHER!

Category: Collectibles:Science:Medicine, Dentistry:Dental

This is a shade matcher for making dentures. Each "tooth" is on a separate pick, collected into a fan-shaped holder. You would hold the "tooth" next to the natural tooth of the patient and get a close match so the dentures looked natural. If you wanted to be really bizarre, you could use the picks in the olives at your next cocktail party!

Location . . . . **Mid-Missouri**
Starting Bid **$7.99**
# of Bids **0**
Selling Price . . . . **No Sale**

Item #5515980940

WISDOM TEETH

Category: Everything Else:Medical, Dental:General

A set of an adult (age: 22) male's wisdom teeth. These four babies were yanked out of my mouth around the end of August and have been double wrapped in a plastic bag ever since. The teeth have been soaked in bleach for two days and then in Listerine for another two.

Location . . . . **Snowy Flagstaff, AZ**
Starting Bid **$9.99**
# of Bids **5**
Selling Price **$20.00**

QUESTION FOR SELLER:

> I am an accomplished puppeteer. As we move forward with designs and
> such, I've begun building puppets using human teeth. I'm wondering how
> sharp the roots are, and if you think they're sturdy enough to be shoved
> into a puppet's mouth. Most likely the puppet will be a savage tramp.

Upon inspecting the teeth I see that two of them have big, solid roots on them that don't look like they will break very easily. The last tooth is broken in three parts, but all of them are still strong so I don't know why you couldn't just glue them back together or into the mouth of the puppet.

Item #1425120416
ABE LINCOLN HAIR

Category: Collectibles:Historical:Other Historical Memorabilia

HAIR OF PRESIDENT ABRAHAM LINCOLN, "THE GREAT EMANCIPATOR." Strand protected in ornate gilt double frames. Taken from a lock of Lincoln's hair originally from the personal collection of famous Lincoln collector Fredrick H. Meserve. A beautiful complete and colorful facsimile letter of the original letter from world-famous expert Charles Hamilton accompanies this piece attesting to its authenticity and provenance. Letters of Lincoln average $12,000 to $50,000. You can buy with confidence: I am a Lifetime Member of the Manuscript Society. The Daguerreian (Photographic) Society has bestowed upon me an Honorary Lifetime Membership.

Location	**Grosse Pointe Farms, MI**
Starting Bid	**$1.00**
# of Bids	9
Selling Price	**$133.50**

Item #1000279708
ANTIQUE HUMAN HAIR FROM 1920s

Category: Everything Else:Weird Stuff: Really Weird

This is hair from approximately the 20s and 30s, removed from an antique barber's chair we recently restored. Some dirt particles included, but the trimmings are still intact. They look like long rolls because this antique hair was recovered from the underside of a circular ring that fits on the base of the barber's chair.

Location	**Corvallis, Oregon**
Starting Bid	**$1.00**
# of Bids	1
Selling Price	**$1.00**

Guaranteed Authentic!

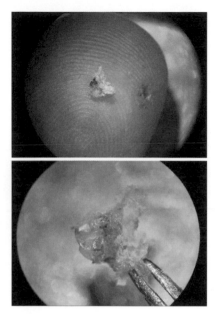

Item #5751140793

MIKE'S WART

Category: Everything Else:General

For the last three or four years, I had this wart on the third finger of my left hand. UNTIL LAST WEEK. Now it can be yours! Yessir, a real honest to goodness wart. Grown right here in the good old U.S. of A.

Location . . . . **Portland, OR**
Starting Bid **$1.00**
# of Bids **0**
Selling Price . . . . **No Sale**

Item #5733769017

MY BIG TOENAIL

Category: Everything Else:General

The winning bidder gets my big toenail! Yes, it's for real. It came off as a result of a sports injury, and now it can be yours to do with as you please. Here are just a few ideas for you:

• It would make a great gag gift!

• Contains actual human DNA—perfect for all of your cloning experiments.

• Attach it to a stick and use it as a back scratcher!

• Attach a handle and turn it into a spoon. A small spoon, of course. But suitable for children.

Location . . . . **Dayton, Ohio**
Starting Bid **$1.00**
# of Bids **0**
Selling Price . . . . **No Sale**

*photos you receive will not contain this blue stripe

Item #1000261485

MY COLON

Category: Everything Else;Weird Stuff: Totally Bizarre

What you're bidding on is a set of two pictures taken in March 1999, via colonoscopy, of my very own colon. Bright and shiny, clean as a whistle, and healthy (so the doctor tells me). You're seeing the "tail end" of the digestive system as you've probably never seen it—from the inside! Odd and eerie, frightening and fascinating, if you stare at the yellow one long enough, you might start to see the vague image of saints, the way some people have seen the image of Mary in the marks on a tortilla. (This, however, is not guaranteed. You see what you see. I see what I see.)

My name on the pic has been blacked out, to make it easier to replace with your own name, or the name of your favorite pain in the a**. Each shot is about 3" by 2¼". Both pics are on one strip, printed (as noted on the back) on Sony print paper.

I know that the starting price may sound a little high, but—hey—if you had to go through what I went through to get these pics, you'd probably be asking a he** of a lot more!

Makes a great gift for that "special someone," or frame it and keep it as your own. Would even make a great picture for this year's Christmas card! I guarantee that your friends and family won't get another card like it!

Location	The Nutmeg State
Starting Bid	$9.99
# of Bids	0
Selling Price	No Sale

RARE VIEW!

This is me!

Sick!!!

BUTT-LIGHT

Category: **Everything Else:General**

Location...... **Mishugineville**
Starting Bid.............. **$7.50**

# of Bids................................**0**
Selling Price......... **No Sale**

DESCRIPTION:

All of 25 centimeters (10 inches), as marked on the side! This is a rigid sigmoidoscope. It is new, made of sturdy clear and white plastic and sealed in a plastic wrapper. The light source is not included. In the old times (just a few years ago) they used to use these rigid babies to check for polyps in the sigmoid colon, that is above rectum. Nowadays they use flexible gizmos connected to a TV, so both the patient and the doctor can relax and enjoy the view all the way up to 60 centimeters. But this is now and that was then. The patient was usually quite unhappy and the doctor was on his knees with his eye at the peephole.

* This is one of the best Valentine gag-gifts I could think of. Can you imagine the expression on his/her face?!! Be careful though, if they don't have a sense of humor you may end up with a free colonoscopy right there!

* It blows great bubbles, so your kids would love it. They could take it to school for show and tell!
* You can use it as a blowgun (now don't get any sick ideas!) that shoots round candy balls. Great favor for your office party!
* It works as a cigar holder too. Give it to your boss as a birthday present and tell him where to stick it with that cigar!
* It works as a seed planter too: Stick it into soft ground to desired depth as marked on the side, pull out the obturator (that thingy that goes inside), and drop your seed into the tube. Then pull out the planter and you are done! Do you think I should advertise it in an infomercial on a home and garden show?
www.naughtytools.com

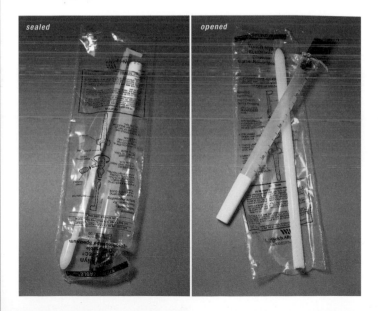

STRYCHNINE PILLS FOR CONSTIPATION!

Category: **Antiques & Art:Medical**

Location **Cincinnati, Ohio**	# of Bids..................................8
Starting Bid.....................**$9.99**	Selling Price **$26.00**

DESCRIPTION:

This is a VERY EARLY patent medicine! Calomel (mercury) is also listed! Now that's just what every constipated person needed! Strychnine was used medically for many years. Like so many medicines, in small doses it was quite useful. In large doses it could be harmful. Contents are sold only for collector purposes and must not be used in any way!

click for larger photo

French sophistication!

front, closed

Item #1415208663

19TH-CENTURY ENEMA MACHINE

Category: Antiques & Art: Medical

Here is an antique probably Victorian-era metal automatic enema machine. It is spring-loaded and is engineered differently than all of the other ones I have seen. Instead of a wind-up type, which is more prone to failure, this one is a simple spring mechanism. It is about 10 and ¾ inches tall. There is an inlet/outlet port at the top where a hose of some type connected. I think the water or medicine was drawn up via this hose by pulling up on the top. Then the fluid is automatically dispelled under pressure. I oould bo wrong but thio io how it appears to work. There are some dents on the body. This does not affect the function or cause leakage and is minor

Location . . . . **Houcton, Toxac**
Starting Bid **$9.99**
# of Bids 25
Selling Price **$134.50**

back, opened

Item #1220520647

PRETTY PLUNGER!

Category: Home & Garden:Home Furnishings:Furnishings:Bathroom

Just when you think you have seen it all! Now here's a plunger that you
don't have to hide, but rather becomes a welcomed, decorating accessory.
And, if placed in a guest bath . . . what a conversation piece! This plunger
has been hand painted and signed by the artist. It is absolutely durable and
waterproof as it is protected with multiple brushed-on coats of polyurethane.
It is meant to be fully functional! If the rubber end becomes less than
beautiful, just go to your local hardware store and buy a replacement cup.

Location . . . . **Rockport, MA**
Starting Bid **$24.99**
# of Bids **0**
Selling Price . . . . **No Sale**

✉ QUESTION FOR SELLER: ◀

> Did you paint this yourself? Is the artist famous in
> any art circles? I had a friend who stealthily painted
> public toilets.

I own a small artisan's shop here in Rockport, MA, and
these things are selling like the proverbial hot cakes.
People even give me wallpaper samples to have them
customized. And yes, I am the artist. Most of the work that
I do is on canes/walking sticks, so these just seemed like
a natural overflow (ha, ha) of painting on that shape.

Item #1000262876
FOSSIL DINOSAUR POOP

Category: Collectibles:Animal:
Dinosaur:Fossils

This is a genuine specimen of mammal dinosaur poop, 60 million years old, found in the Utah area with other dinosaur bones. Size is 1 1/2" long, petrified—I assure you, there's no smell! Great for that special someone! Or just a fossil collector gone amok! Called "coprolite" in polite fossil society. We've traveled in fossil circles many years. We have purchased prehistoric material (bone, shell, coprolite, footprint casts) from reputable excavators of these materials from known fossil digs in the U.S. and overseas. We know when we're handling the real McCoy. Our credibility is extremely important to us—we don't even handle artificially colored gemstones in our store. If we didn't know our stuff we'd be in big doo-doo (no pun intended). tellmewhereonearth.com

Location	**Nevada**
Starting Bid	**$5.99**
# of Bids	0
Selling Price	**No Sale**

Item #5572624463
MOOSE POOP

Category: Everything Else!:
Rock/Fossil/Mineral:General

Yes, you read right, I have a single moose poop nugget for sale, and yes . . . it's real! Comes in an attractive gift box. The poop is approximately 3/4 inch long and is quite hard, non-staining (if kept dry), and a hell of a conversation piece! I collected this on a nature hike up in the woods behind where my parents live in Vermont. For some strange reason I brought it home (I live in North Carolina). I've just had it sitting in a drawer since then (why, I don't really KNOW why!) and it's now a petrified poop! Buyer to pay actual shitting (oops, I meant SHIPPING) charges. Happy Bidding!!! :)

Location	**Greenville, NC**
Starting Bid	**$.25**
# of Bids	4
Selling Price	**$2.00**

Genuine!

DEER POOP PAPERWEIGHT

Category: **Sports:Sporting Goods:Hiking**

Location............**New England**
Starting Bid.................. **$6.95**

# of Bids...................................**1**
Selling Price............ **$6.95**

DESCRIPTION:

Genuine preserved whitetail deer droppings in a crystal glass paperweight. Snow and evergreens added for a natural look. Comes in a gold foil gift box.

✉ **QUESTION FOR SELLER:**

> Do you know where the poop was found? I'm a collector of animal
> droppings from around the world, and I'm curious
> as to whether this poop comes from an area I'm
> targeting. Also, is it a good, sturdy paperweight?

I have Massachusetts and Maine whitetail deer poop.
The bottom of the paperweight is a heavy felt. I also
have wild turkey poop (MA) and porcupine poop (ME).

click for larger photo

CANNED DEER DUNG

Category: **Collectibles:Animal:Wildlife**

Location........**Saskatchewan**

Starting Bid..........**$4.99**

# of Bids.................................**0**

Seller Rating..............**2048**

DESCRIPTION:

Not sure about a city that gives deer dung as a souvenir, but it is a novel way of getting rid of your sewage. A can of genuine fossilized deer droppings, still unopened, unreserved.

✉ **QUESTION FOR SELLER:**

> Hello. I recently saw a woman on eBay selling paperweights made
> from deer doo. Do you suppose I could make my own paperweights

> with these droppings? What about other crafts,
> such as earrings or airplanes? I live in New York. We
> should sell pigeon droppings. We've always got
> dumb tourists here. Thank you!

I don't know as the can has never been opened. I got
it with a package deal so I never bought it as such.

click for larger photo

Item #1609972831

PENIS-SHAPED CHEETO

Category: Everything Else:Novelties:Risqué

When I was pregnant last year I had an overwhelming craving for Cheetos. There I sat, munching away, when I noticed the most peculiar Cheeto. It was shaped like a penis! This is a very detailed Cheeto— looks like a set of meat AND potatoes. I have plenty of bubblewrap so I will package it really well to keep the little fellow safe. Mind you, this Cheeto is over a year old so some of his cheesiness is fading. Still has a lovely cheddar patina though.

Location . . . . **Tulsa**
Starting Bid **$1.00**
# of Bids 2
Selling Price **$1.25**

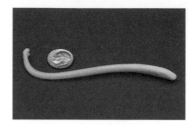

Item #1000254593

RACCOON WINKIE BONE

Category: Everything Else:Weird Stuff: Totally Bizarre

I recently found and bought a small collection of raccoon penis bones. Yes, a few lucky mammals actually have penis bones allowing them to perform regardless of stress at work and/or how much they drank at the singles bar before getting lucky. All of these range from 3–4". If you are an animal rights activist, don't worry. None of these came from live raccoons. All were shot, trapped, and/or clubbed to death first.

Location . . . . **Montana**
Starting Bid **$10.00**
# of Bids 1
Selling Price **$10.00**

Item #1157455022

POTTED PENIS PLANTS SCULPTURE!

Category: Collectibles:Art, Animation & Photo Images: Art:Artistic Nudes

Nice piece of art. Makes a great gift for your favorite penis fan or plant lover.

Location . . . . **Coral Springs, FL**
Starting Bid **$9.95**
# of Bids 1
Selling Price **$9.95**

Item #1115534792

BED PAN URINAL COMBO

Category: Collectibles:Medicine, Dentistry: Other Items

This is an old piece of hospital equipment, the stuff before plastic! I believe this is a piece of porcelain and it is marked "Thompson" on the bottom. It is heavy and in perfect condition.

Location .... **The Natural State**
Starting Bid **$19.99**
# of Bids 0
Selling Price .... No Sale

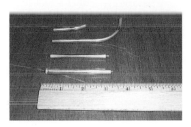

Item #1900114287

CIVIL WAR MEDICAL CATHETER

Category: Science, Medical:Other Science Collectibles

This is a four-piece Civil War male & female catheter. It could be used also on a child. Made of nickel silver-plated brass. These were carried in a surgeon's pocket kit and would be screwed together to fit the patient's needs.

Location .... **Florida**
Starting Bid **$9.99**
# of Bids 3
Selling Price **$20.50**

Item #1000333037

MEDICAL CASTRATION TOOL

Category: Everything Else:Weird Stuff: Totally Bizarre

An old tool that was used down on the farm for castrating those farm critters. It has some surface corrosion, so I would be sure to scrub it down good before doing any serious castratin'.

Location .... **Western New York**
Starting Bid **$15.00**
# of Bids 1
Selling Price **$15.00**

BULL PENIS CANE

Category: **Everything Else**

Location	**Sandy, Utah**	# of Bids	**0**
Starting Bid	**$74.99**	Selling Price	**No Sale**

DESCRIPTION:

This is an absolutely unique, one-of-a-kind walking stick or cane with a brass doorknob handle, handmade from the reproductive organ of a bull. The man who makes these sterilizes them, dries them out, puts a steel rod down the center, and then highly varnishes them. Measures 36½ inches tall. You can have it personalized on the grip with a name plate for ten dollars extra.

✉ QUESTION FOR SELLER:

click for larger photo

> That's a heckuva penis. I'd like to make a pinwheel
> out of it. Is this something that can be placed on
> some type of mounting device?

Yes, you are correct. There's no reason you couldn't create a pinwheel out of it.

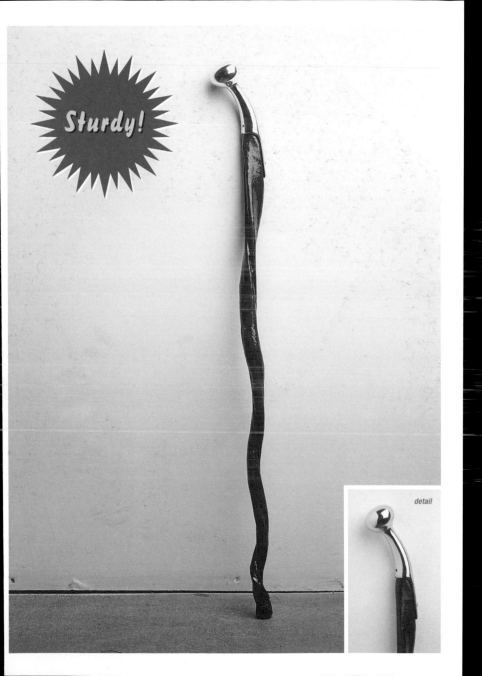

Sturdy!

detail

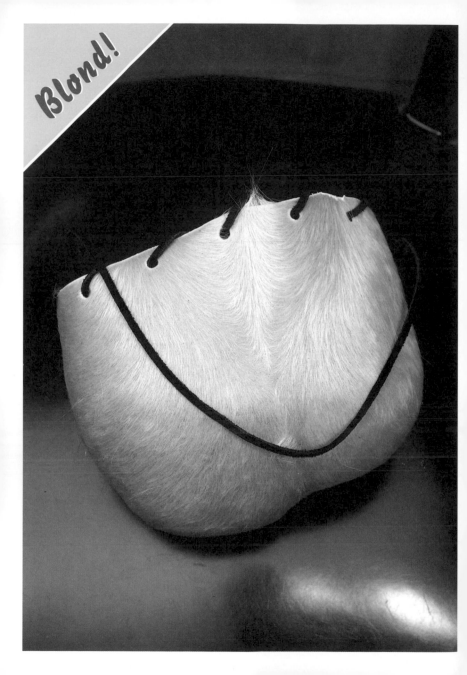

Blond!

Item #1221081287

BULL SCROTUM BAG

Category: **Home & Garden:Home Furnishings:Furnishings:General**

Location........ **El Paso, Texas**	# of Bids.................................**1**
Starting Bid............ **$30.00**	Selling Price........ **$30.00**

DESCRIPTION:

Bulls don't think this is much of a good-luck charm, but some folks think it's a sign of fertility. I think it's a great gag gift, a wonderful conversation piece. And it has hundreds of uses. Please be advised that colors, shapes, and sizes vary widely.

✉ QUESTION FOR SELLER:

> Hello! Will this hold up okay if I serve fruit in it? Also, what do
> you do with the testicles?

Yeah, I don't see any reason why not, since the bags are tanned. Keep in mind that they should be kept dry. Great for walnuts, I suppose! The testicles go to restaurants. Mountain oysters they are called. I don't like them. They taste rather fatty and cost like hell.

click for larger photo

Item #5927199287

1972 AMC: GREMLIN

Category: Passenger Vehicles:AMC:All Models

This Gremlin has 42,700 miles, is originally from Iowa, was always garage kept, and runs great. It has new tires and battery. The interior looks brand new and is navy blue plaid. The outside paint is still shiny white. Send seller email for more pictures!

Location . . . . **Arlington, TX**
Starting Bid **$1,500**
# of Bids **1**
Selling Price . . . . **Reserve not met**

Item #5928337449

1953 FORD GOLDEN JUBILEE TRACTOR W/3 POINT

Category: Everything Else

1953 FORD GOLDEN JUBILEE TRACTOR with three point. This is an incredible find for the vintage Ford tractor collector. I am selling this tractor for a good friend of mine who is selling off his excess equipment. It is in very good original condition. It is a four-speed with high-low range and runs very good. The three-point is very strong, and the rear tires are in very good condition. It also has a PTO belt pulley attachment. There is a possible serial number located on the transmission housing by the starter of AA5606l with a diamond symbol immediately after the number.

Location . . . . **Fort Phillipsburg**
Starting Bid **$2,999.00**
# of Bids 1
Selling Price $2,999.00

Item #4512436473

SPIDERMAN PT CRUISER

Category: Passenger Vehicles:Customized

The vehicles have been airbrushed by various American artists, and come signed and numbered making these super cars absolutely unique! You will also receive a certificate of authenticity showing that you have the number (#) in a series of one-of-a kind vehicles. www.ttaeventworks.com

Location . . . . **Florida**
Starting Bid **$1.00**
# of Bids 8
Selling Price $29,800

Item #5929070022

CLASSIC 1954 MACK DUMP TRUCK

Category: Motors:Other Vehicles: Commercial Trucks

The B Model Mack is recognized world over as THE classic American big truck. This truck has had only one registered owner and the title that comes with it is the 1954 Missouri title showing that this unit, fitted with a mixer body, sold for $59,848.64. Later in its life this truck was fitted with the dump body that it now has. The tail gate is excellent and the dump body is solid, there is no rust out, but some of the welded could stand a little attention. Speedometer shows around 70,000 miles, which is like nothing for a Mack. If you are looking for a classic Mack, here is your chance to get one. 25% down payment is expected. Reasonable shipping can be arranged, if required.

Location . . . . **Hartsville, TN**
Starting Bid **$99.00**
# of Bids **20**
Selling Price **$1,025.00**

Not a Lemon!

CONVENIENCE STORE

Category: **Real Estate:Commercial:Other**

Location.................. **Killen, Ala.**
Starting Bid...... **$129,000.00**

# of Bids.. **0**
Selling Price.......... **No Sale**

DESCRIPTION:

This 3600 sq. ft. property has a concrete block building on a concrete slab. Once used as a convenience store with deli. There are two underground gas tanks that are up to current standards. The building has electric a.c. and gas heat. The roof is new, replaced 1 year ago. This area is growing and is an excellent location for a restaurant or deli. Currently there is a rental lot for a mobile home behind the store. It is rented at this time.

click for larger photo

Item #1000359262
FIREWOOD

Category: Home & Garden

Completely brand new. Okay, unused. Well anyway, it is good-looking Colorado firewood from genuine Colorado trees! I'm almost willing to give it away to the first person with a truck who shows up in my driveway!! NOTE: YOU do have to pick up. No shipping on this. It wouldn't be possible! NO JOKE: FIREWOOD FOR YOUR FIREPLACE!!

Location . . . . **Denver, Colorado**
Starting Bid **$1.00**
# of Bids 3
Selling Price **$1.25**

Item #1124754784
1 WOODEN LEG, 1 UNFINISHED WHITTLING

Category: Antiques & Art:Medical

Two old wooden legs. One has metal joints, still moves freely, & has leather strapping. The other is a partially carved leg, still in its whittling stage.

Location . . . . **Catskills**
Starting Bid **$9.99**
# of Bids 6
Selling Price **$51.00**

QUESTION FOR SELLER:

> I lost the lower portion of my leg in a bizarre billiards incident (my
> lawyer says not to talk about it). Anyway, this looks like a cheap, temp-
> orary fix. The stains look like bruises, and that oughta get me some
> sympathy from the chicks. Girls dig bruises. Is this still in working order?

Sorry to hear about the billiards incident, I hate when that happens. I am posting the leg for a person here in town. He got the leg from an old barn storage. Neither of us is sure how old it may be.

Item #1649817800

UNKNOWN CARVED LADY ON PIECE OF THIN BARK TREE

Category: Art:Folk Art

I don't know much about this except that it was given to me by an old friend who spent a lot of time in forests. It's a pretty nice carving.

Location . . . . **Texas**
Starting Bid **$0.50**
# of Bids 1
Selling Price **$0.50**

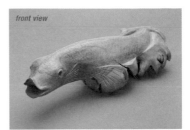
front view

bottom view

Item #1649910336

FISH CARVED FROM FUNGUS

Category: Everything Else:Weird Stuff: Really Weird

Someone put some real work into this one! It's a real piece of tree fungus carved into some sort of fish or scary sea creature. Truly one of a kind. Makes an unusual gift.

Location . . . . **Mercer, PA**
Starting Bid **$1.00**
# of Bids 1
Selling Price **$6.00**

Buy it now!

WHITTLED FROM A VERMONT FENCE

Category: **Everything Else**

Location **Plainfield, Vermont**
Starting Bid **$4.00**

# of Bids 1
Selling Price **$4.00**

DESCRIPTION:

I am told, by my 93-year-old advisor, that this item is a wooden flask that was whittled from a wooden fence post here in Vermont. He says it may also have been used as a vase. Presently it does not hold water; that is, age has rendered it incapable of this function. However, it makes one heck of a conversation piece or can be used to hold a dried flower or two, or three. Measures 3½" at its widest point, and 6¼" tall.

click for larger photo

Item #1000358220

NOTHING!
ABSOLUTELY NOTHING!

Category: **Everything Else**

Location............**Sedalia, MO**	# of Bids...............................6
Starting Bid.......................**$.01**	Selling Price............**$1.03**

DESCRIPTION:

I am selling absolutely nothing. Shipping charges are also absolutely nothing. If you would like to see the nothing that I am selling, it looks sort of like this picture. I'm not sure what you can do with it. Anything you want to, I guess, or nothing at all.

✉ QUESTION FOR SELLER:

> If I bid on your auction, what will you do with the
> money? Thank you very much for all your help.

I figured if I made any sort of substantial amount that I would donate it to the Percussive Arts Society at my school, Central Missouri State University. They are in dire need of new percussion instruments.

click for larger photo

🙂	*Positive!*	**Excellent transaction and communication—Highest recommendation and regards**
🙂	*Positive!*	**Perfect Transaction AAAAA+++++++++++++++++**
🙂	*Positive!*	**Very fast email and payment!! A++++++++++++++++++++++Thanks**
🙂	*Positive!*	**VERY FAST PAYMENT!!!!! HIGHLY RECOMMENDED!!!!!!**
🙂	*Positive!*	**Enjoy keeping your hands clean, 1970s style! A+ buyer!**
🙂	*Positive!*	**FAST PAY, GOOD EMAILS, SMOOTH TRANSACTION. RECOMMEND THIS BUYER!!!**
🙂	*Positive!*	**Very fast payment, A real credit to eBay, Would definitely sell to again, A+++++**
🙂	*Positive!*	**Prompt payment. Very good to do business with!! A++**
🙂	*Positive!*	**Friendly buyer with lightning fast payment. A++++++**
🙂	*Positive!*	**Prompt payment & good emails...thanks for making eBay work so well!!**
🙂	*Positive!*	**Prompt payment. Very good to do business with!! A++**
🙂	*Positive!*	**Fast payment, a pleasure to do business with. Thanks!**
🙂	*Positive!*	**Great eBayer...Smooth transaction...gladly do again...Thanks**
🙂	*Positive!*	**Super fast payment. Nice guy. Would highly recommend. A+++++++++++**
🙂	*Positive!*	**Fast Money A++**
🙂	*Positive!*	**A pleasure to do business with**
🙂	*Positive!*	**FASTEST PAYER ON EBAY!!**
🙂	*Positive!*	**Fast Payment! Excellent emails! Smooth Deal! Thank you! AAAA++++**
🙂	*Positive!*	**Fast payment and friendly email! Strongly Recommended!**

⚪ 🙂 *Positive!*	Leave feedback for Marc Hartzman	
⚪ 😐 **Neutral**		[**LEAVE FEEDBACK NOW**]
⚪ 🙁 **Negative**		

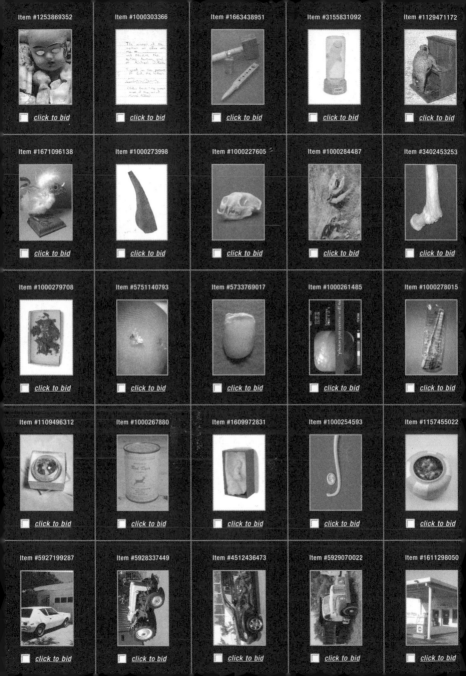

Item #1253869352
click to bid

Item #1000303366
click to bid

Item #1663438951
click to bid

Item #3155831092
click to bid

Item #1129471172
click to bid

Item #1671096138
click to bid

Item #1000273998
click to bid

Item #1000227605
click to bid

Item #1000284487
click to bid

Item #3402453253
click to bid

Item #1000279708
click to bid

Item #5751140793
click to bid

Item #5733769017
click to bid

Item #1000261485
click to bid

Item #1000278015
click to bid

Item #1109496312
click to bid

Item #1000267880
click to bid

Item #1609972831
click to bid

Item #1000254593
click to bid

Item #1157455022
click to bid

Item #5927199287
click to bid

Item #5928337449
click to bid

Item #4512436473
click to bid

Item #5929070022
click to bid

Item #1611298050
click to bid